Level 2 - ❷

W0099658

The War Between the States

Curtis Kelly

Series Editor **Rob Waring**

Level 2-❷

The War Between the States

Curtis Kelly

© 2017 Seed Learning, Inc.

All rights reserved. No part of this book may be reproduced, stored in a retrieval system, or transmitted in any form by any means, electronic, mechanical, photocopying, recording, or otherwise, without prior permission in writing from the publisher.

Series Editor: Rob Waring
Acquisitions Editor: Liana Robinson
Copy Editor: Casey Malarcher
Cover/Interior Design: Andy Roh

ISBN: 978-1-9464-5207-8

10 9 8 7 6 5 4 3 2 1
21 20 19 18 17

Contents

A War That Changed America

This is the story of a war, a deadly war. It was a war that was won with a river. It was a war where about 625,000 people lost their lives. But another 4 million people, black people who were slaves, got a chance to live freely.

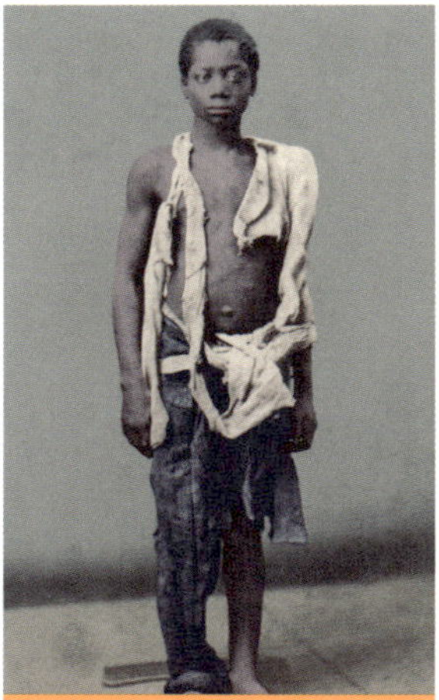
A young slave

North against South

The South Breaks Away

The war started in America in 1861. The South broke away from the North. The states in the South had slaves. The slaves were people brought from Africa. They were owned, bought, and sold like property. They were not paid for their work.

Slaves in the South

Northern and Southern states

Washington
Oregon
Territory
Territory
Dakota
Minnesota
Lake Superior
Wisconsin
Michigan
Lake Michigan
Lake Huron
Lake Ontario
Lake Erie
New York
Maine
Ver-
mont
New
Hamp-
shire
Massachusetts
Connec-
ticut
Rhode Island
Pennsylvania
New Jersey
Delaware
Maryland
Iowa
Illinois
Indiana
Ohio
West
Virginia
Virginia
Kentucky
Missouri
Kansas
Nebraska Territory
Nevada
Territory
Utah
Territory
Colorado
Territory
California
New Mexico
Territory
Indian
Territory
Arkansas
Tennessee
North Carolina
South
Carolina
Georgia
Alabama
Mississippi
Texas
Louisiana
Florida
ATLA
OCEAN
IC
CEAN
MEXICO
Gulf of Mexico
Union states without slavery
Union States with slavery
Confederate States
Territories

A reenactment of the North fighting the South

The North did not want the South to make a new country. So there was a war. It was called the Civil War.

At that time, the United States had 34 states. The war was between the 20 states in the North and the 11 states in the South. Three states were in the middle. They did not want to be in the war.

A Long War

The war went on for four years. It was a terrible war. About 625,000 soldiers died. They died in battles between the North and the South. They also died of disease. Actually, for every soldier killed in battle, two died of disease. It was difficult to keep the soldiers healthy while they were living in camps.

Many soldiers died

The First Battle of Bull Run

The first major battle was in Virginia. It was a place called Bull Run.

Soldiers

The soldiers from the South waited. The soldiers from the North attacked them. They fought against each other all day. The North was winning.

Then more Southern soldiers arrived by train. The South started attacking. They started winning. Some soldiers from the North began to run away. Then more ran. The South won the battle.

The First Battle of Bull Run

General Robert E. Lee

In 1862, Robert E. Lee was put in charge of an army for the South. He was one of the best soldiers of his time. His army became the most famous and most successful of the Southern armies.

General Robert E. Lee

A reenactment showing Southern soldiers

Controlling the Mississippi River

During the war, the Mississippi River was very important. Soldiers and food were sent up and down the river quickly. The river went through many of the Southern states.

The North wanted to control the river. By controlling the river, they could cut the South in two. Southern soldiers on one side of the river would not be able to help Southern soldiers on the other side of the river. Slowly, the North took control. Army and navy soldiers worked together fighting battles.

A farm with slaves

The US Gunship Cairo built for the navy

The capture of Fort Henry by the North

The Battle for Vicksburg

The South had an important river fortress at Vicksburg. It was high above the river and hard to get to. The North attacked many times but could not win.

Then one of the generals from the North, General Grant, got an idea. He put his soldiers around the city and waited. After 46 days, the soldiers in the city did not have any food. They let Grant come into the city. The North won the battle.

General Grant

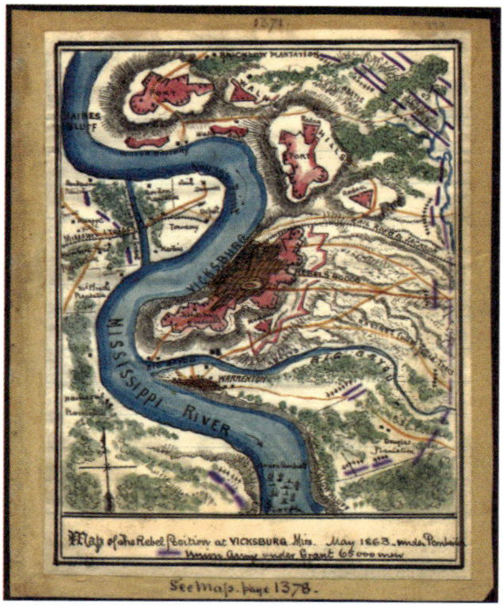

HAINES BLUFF
FORT
FORT
HILL
VICKSBURG
WARRENTON
BIG BAYOU
MISSISSIPPI RIVER
Map of the Rebel Position at VICKSBURG Miss. May 1863
See Map. page 1378.

Vicksburg and the Mississippi River

Fighting at Vicksburg

After taking Vicksburg, the North won another important battle. This was the Battle of Gettysburg. Together, these battles were the turning point in the war.

Most of the fighting during the war was in the South. But Gettysburg was a battle fought in the North.

A civil war ship

Gettysburg

General Lee moved north with his army and attacked. The battle lasted three days. Many soldiers were hurt, died, or went missing—as many as 51,000 soldiers!

A statue of a Northern soldier, Gettysburg

A reenactment of the Battle of Gettysburg

The War Ends

By the end of the war, the North had many more soldiers than the South. The South could not fight them. The North was too strong. The South stopped the war. The North won.

Many men died.

A reenactment of the end of the war

President Abraham Lincoln frees the slaves.

In the beginning, the war was fought to keep the North and South together as one country. But as the war continued, it also became about freedom. President Lincoln made laws against slavery. It was illegal. There were no more slaves.

AM I NOT A MAN AND A BROTHER?

A poster against slavery

Slaves wanted to be free.

Slaves go to Northern soldiers.

No slave wanted to be a slave. During the war, slaves would run to the Northern soldiers. They would see the soldiers and ask for protection and freedom.

A young slave asking for protection

Soldiers during a battle

In 1862, President Lincoln let black people become soldiers for the North. They fought to make their friends and families free.

Proud soldiers who fought for the North

Now, in the United States, all people live together and are free. They are all Americans.

Comprehension Questions

1. How were the North and South different?
   (a) The North had slaves.
   (b) The South had slaves.
   (c) The South had more states.
   (d) The North had a new name.

2. What did the South want to do?
   (a) Change the North
   (b) Make friends with the North
   (c) Stop having slaves
   (d) Make a new country

3. Who won the First Battle of Bull Run?
   (a) The North
   (b) The South
   (c) Both the North and the South
   (d) Neither the North nor the South

4. Who was Robert E. Lee?
   (a) A slave
   (b) The president of the US
   (c) A general for the North
   (d) A general for the South

5. Why did the North want to control the Mississippi river?
   (a) To get more soldiers
   (b) To make the South weak
   (c) To get more slaves
   (d) To have water to drink

6. Which two battles were the turning point in the war?
   (a) Bull Run and Vicksburg
   (b) Gettysburg and Grant
   (c) Vicksburg and Gettysburg
   (d) Grant and Bull Run

7. What did President Lincoln do?
   (a) Fought as a soldier
   (b) Made slavery illegal
   (c) Helped the South
   (d) Became president after the war

8. The slaves did NOT want…
   (a) freedom.
   (b) protection.
   (c) to be slaves.
   (d) to fight for the North.

9. Who won the war?
   (a) The North
   (b) The South
   (c) The slaves
   (d) General Lee

10. These days, all Americans…
    (a) are soldiers.
    (b) live in the South.
    (c) have slaves.
    (d) are free.

Key **1.** (b) **2.** (d) **3.** (b) **4.** (d) **5.** (b) **6.** (c) **7.** (b) **8.** (c) **9.** (a) **10.** (d)

Glossary

- **Africa** the continent south of Europe
- **attack** to make a sudden, violent attempt to hurt or damage
- **battle** a fight between two armies in a war
- **freedom** the right to live without being controlled by anyone else
- **freely** able to do things without being controlled
- **fortress** a large, strong building or group of buildings that can be defended from attack
- **general** a very important leader of soldiers
- **Mississippi River** a river that goes north to south across the United States
- **President Abraham Lincoln** the 16th president of the United States
- **slave** a person who is owned by someone else and must work for them
- **soldier** a person in an army
- **state** a part of a country
- **the United States** America; the country between Canada and Mexico

Image Credit/Pages

©Shutterstock: front cover, back cover, 1, 4, 5, 6, 7, 8, 9, 11 middle, 12, 13, 14, 15, 16, 17
Wikipedia: 10 bottom left
Library of Congress: 10 bottom right, 11 bottom

World History Timeline

This chart shows a rough overview of world history.
Some of the dates have been simplified.

World History Timeline

3000 BC | 2900 BC | 2800 BC | 2700 BC | 2600 BC | 2500 BC

Narmer, Egyptian King
(c. 3000 BC)

Pyramids of Giza
(built c. 2550-2490 BC)

Cuneiform (c. 3000 BC-100 AD)

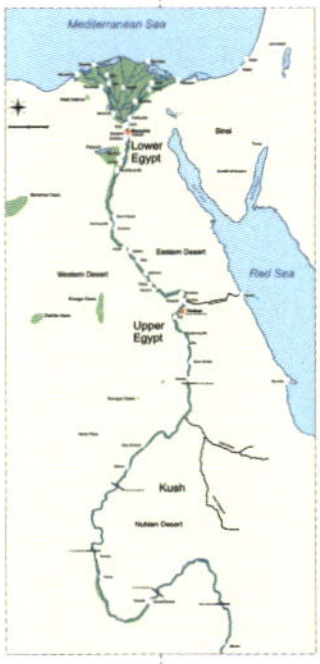
Mediterranean Sea
Lower Egypt
Upper Egypt
Red Sea
Kush
Old Egyptian Kingdom (c. 2686 BC)

2900 BC | 2800 BC | 2700 BC | 2600 BC | 2500 BC

← 5000 BC Mesopotamia (Sumerians)

← 3100 BC Early Dynastic Period of Egypt | Old Egyptian Kingdom

← 3650 BC Minoan Civilization (Crete)

Early Bronze Age

3000 BC | 2900 BC | 2800 BC | 2700 BC | 2600 BC | 2500 BC

2400 BC | 2300 BC | 2200 BC | 2100 BC | 2000 BC

Sahure, Egyptian King
(c. 2487-2475 BC)

Indus Valley
Civilization

Sargon the Great,
Akkadian King
(c. 2340-2284 BC)

Gudea of Lagash
(c. 2144-2124 BC)

Ebla
Tuttul
Amorites
Mari
Amorites
Assur
Arbela
UR III EMPIRE
Sippar
Akshak
Babylon
Kish
Nippur
Larak
Der
Shuruppak
Umma
Lagash
Ur
ELAM
Susa

Ur III Dynasty (c. 2112-2004 BC)

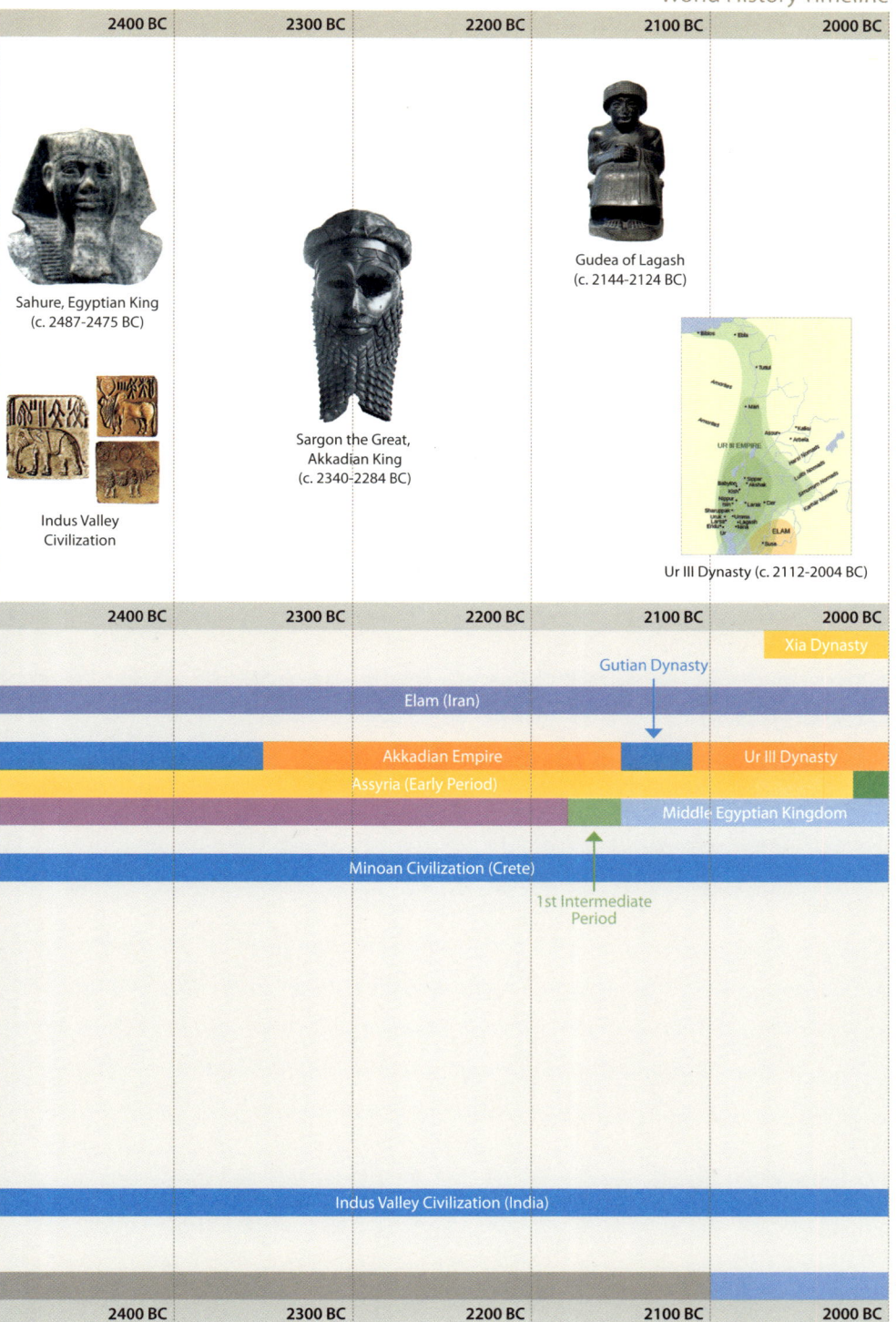

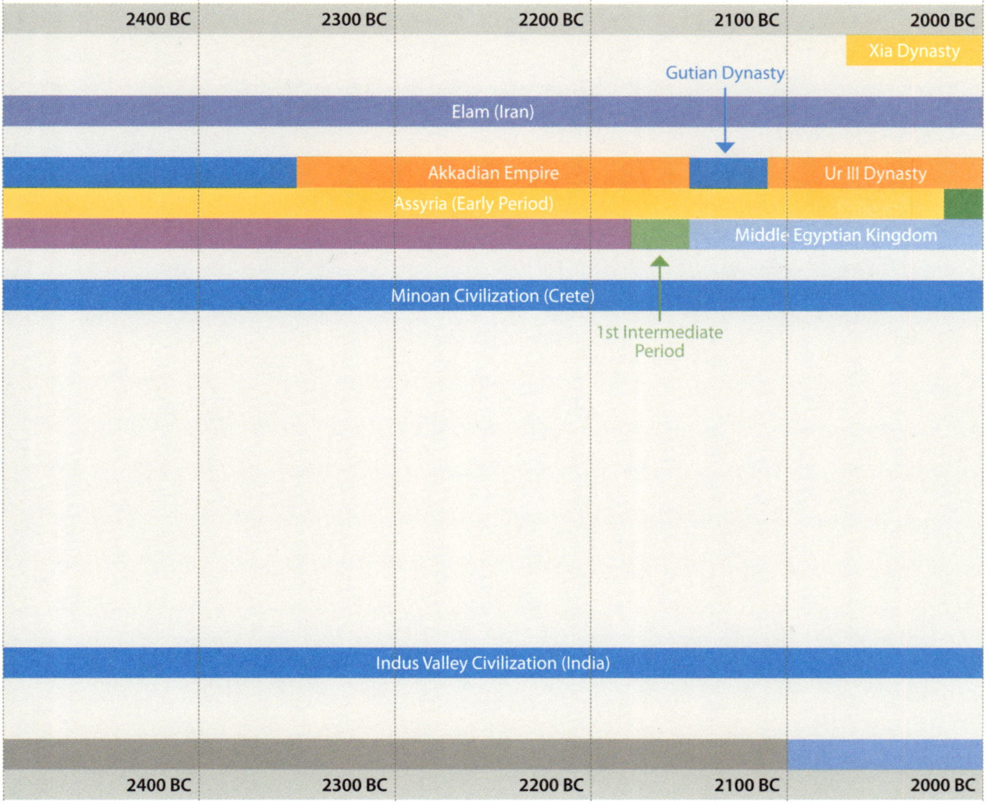
2400 BC
2300 BC
2200 BC
2100 BC
2000 BC
Xia Dynasty
Gutian Dynasty
Elam (Iran)
Akkadian Empire
Ur III Dynasty
Assyria (Early Period)
Middle Egyptian Kingdom
Minoan Civilization (Crete)
1st Intermediate Period
Indus Valley Civilization (India)
2400 BC
2300 BC
2200 BC
2100 BC
2000 BC

World History Timeline

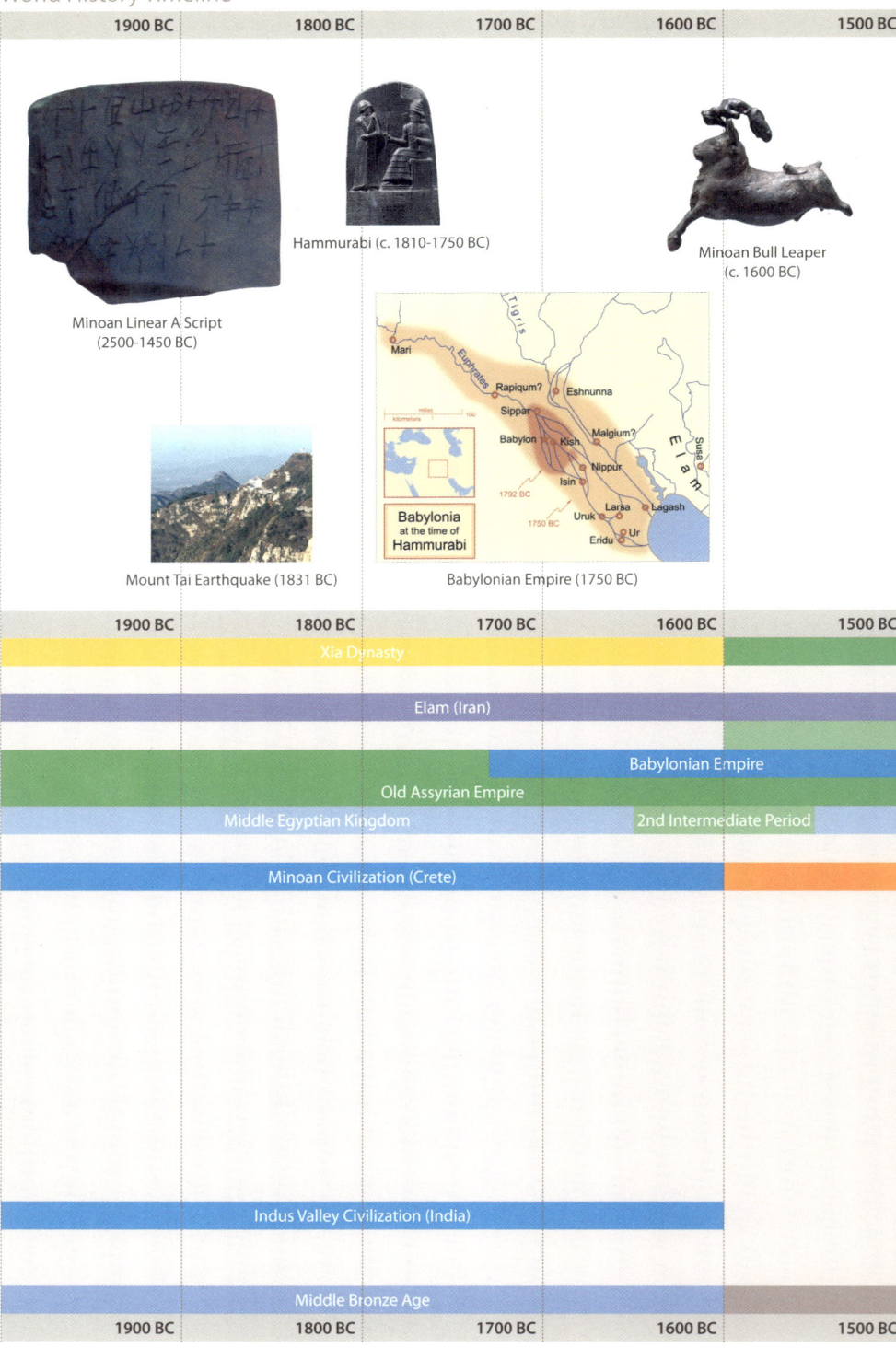

1900 BC | 1800 BC | 1700 BC | 1600 BC | 1500 BC

Minoan Linear A Script (2500-1450 BC)

Hammurabi (c. 1810-1750 BC)

Minoan Bull Leaper (c. 1600 BC)

Mount Tai Earthquake (1831 BC)

Tigris
Mari
Euphrates
Rapiqum?
Eshnunna
Sippar
Babylon
Kish
Malgium?
Elam
Susa
Nippur
Isin
1792 BC
Uruk
Larsa
Lagash
1750 BC
Ur
Eridu
Babylonia at the time of Hammurabi

Babylonian Empire (1750 BC)

1900 BC | 1800 BC | 1700 BC | 1600 BC | 1500 BC

Xia Dynasty

Elam (Iran)

Babylonian Empire

Old Assyrian Empire

Middle Egyptian Kingdom

2nd Intermediate Period

Minoan Civilization (Crete)

Indus Valley Civilization (India)

Middle Bronze Age

1900 BC | 1800 BC | 1700 BC | 1600 BC | 1500 BC

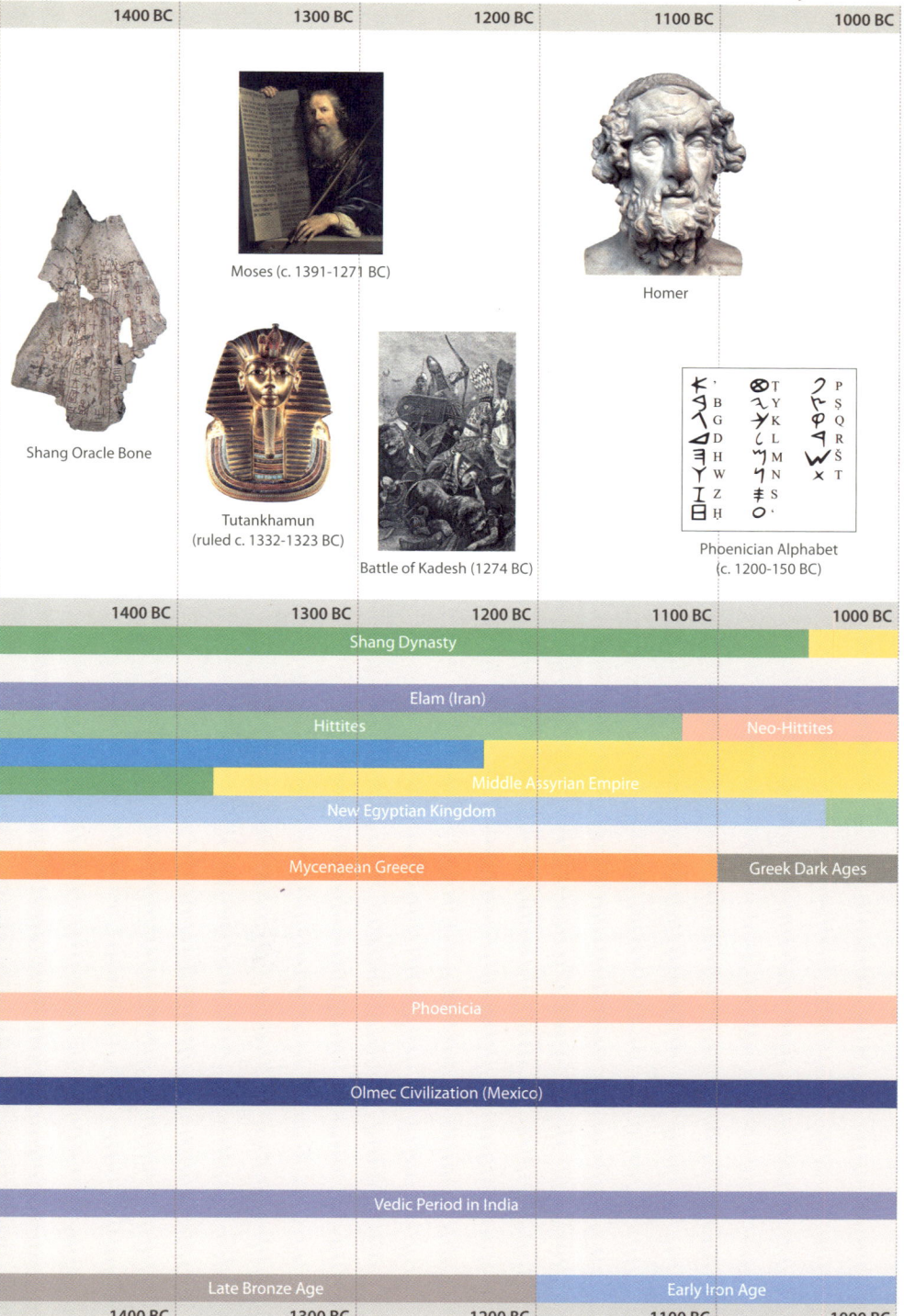

1400 BC	1300 BC	1200 BC	1100 BC	1000 BC

Shang Oracle Bone

Moses (c. 1391-1271 BC)

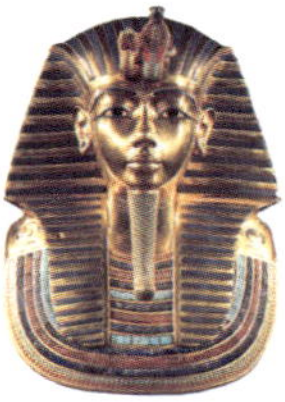

Tutankhamun
(ruled c. 1332-1323 BC)

Battle of Kadesh (1274 BC)

Homer

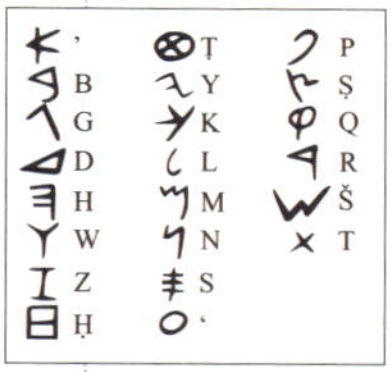

' B G D H W Z Ḥ
T Y K L M N S '
P Ṣ Q R Š T

Phoenician Alphabet
(c. 1200-150 BC)

1400 BC	1300 BC	1200 BC	1100 BC	1000 BC

Shang Dynasty

Elam (Iran)

Hittites — Neo-Hittites

Middle Assyrian Empire

New Egyptian Kingdom

Mycenaean Greece — Greek Dark Ages

Phoenicia

Olmec Civilization (Mexico)

Vedic Period in India

Late Bronze Age — Early Iron Age

1400 BC	1300 BC	1200 BC	1100 BC	1000 BC

World History Timeline

900 BC 800 BC 700 BC 600 BC 500 BC

Zhou Bronze Vessel
(c. 1000 BC)

First Ancient
Olympics (776 BC)

Darius the Great
(550-486 BC)

Olmec Colossal Head

Black Sea
Scythians
Greek
City States
Phrygian
Kingdom
Urartu
Caspian Sea
Mediterranean Sea
Libyans
The Egyptian
Kingdom
(before 671 B.C.)
Red Sea
Persian Gulf
Assyrian Empire – 824 B.C.
Assyrian Empire – 671 B.C.

Neo-Assyrian Empire (911–609 BC)

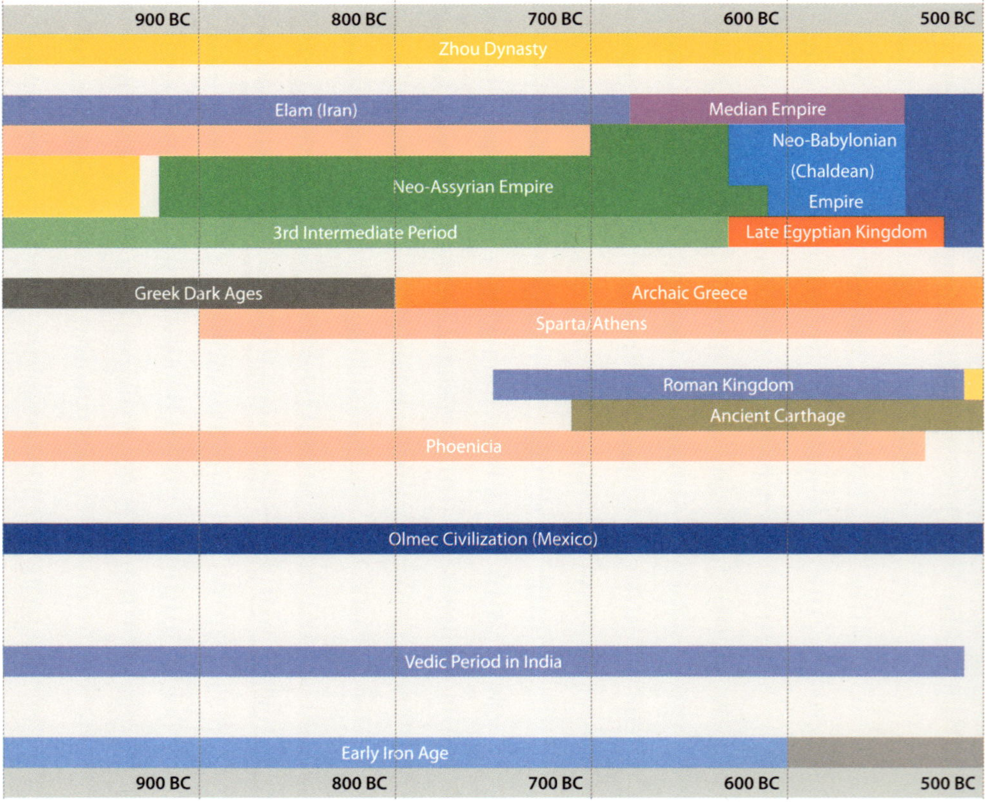
900 BC
800 BC
700 BC
600 BC
500 BC
Zhou Dynasty
Elam (Iran)
Median Empire
Neo-Babylonian
(Chaldean)
Empire
Neo-Assyrian Empire
3rd Intermediate Period
Late Egyptian Kingdom
Greek Dark Ages
Archaic Greece
Sparta/Athens
Roman Kingdom
Ancient Carthage
Phoenicia
Olmec Civilization (Mexico)
Vedic Period in India
Early Iron Age

400 BC | 300 BC | 200 BC | 100 BC | 0

Battle of Salamis
(480 BC)

Alexander the Great
(356-323 BC)

Hannibal
(247-183 BC)

Julius Caesar
(100-44 BC)

Cleopatra
(69-30 BC)

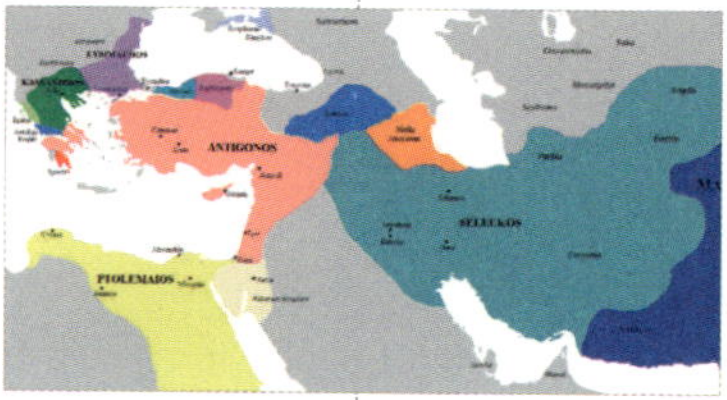

Seleucid Empire (312-63 BC)

Rossetta Stone
(created 196 BC)

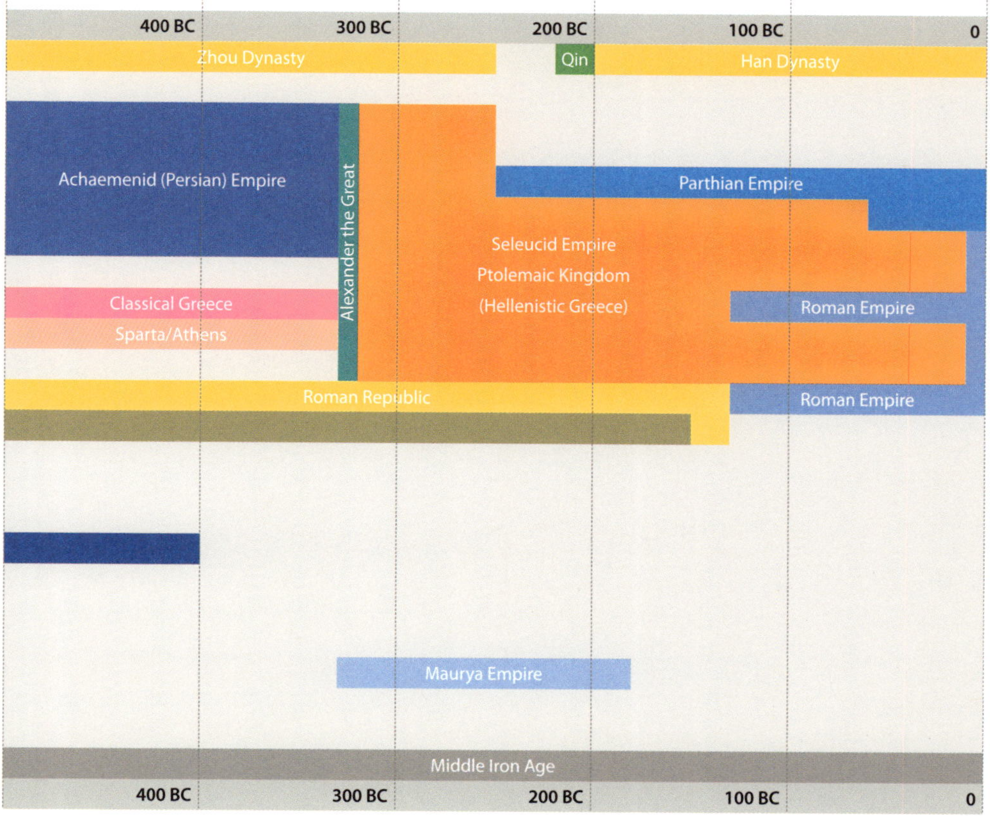
400 BC
300 BC
200 BC
100 BC
0
Zhou Dynasty
Qin
Han Dynasty
Achaemenid (Persian) Empire
Alexander the Great
Parthian Empire
Seleucid Empire
Ptolemaic Kingdom
(Hellenistic Greece)
Classical Greece
Sparta/Athens
Roman Empire
Roman Republic
Roman Empire
Maurya Empire
Middle Iron Age
400 BC
300 BC
200 BC
100 BC
0

World History Timeline

100 | 200 | 300 | 400 | 500

Jesus Christ
(c. 4 BC-30 AD)

Colosseum (built 70-80)

Printing with Wooden Blocks in China (220)

Attila the Hun
(c. 406-453)

117 AD

Roman Empire

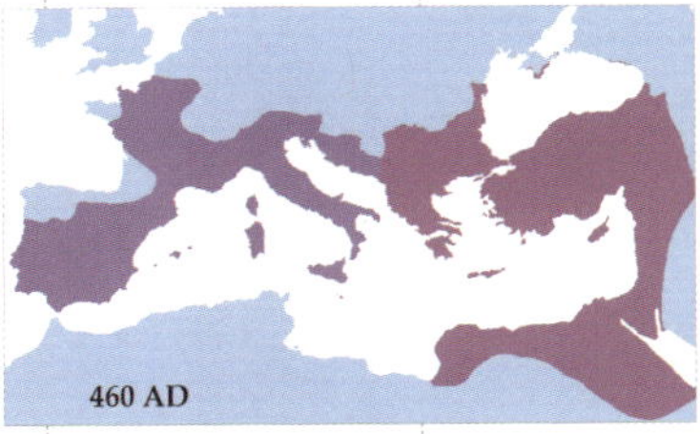
460 AD

Eastern Roman Empire/Western Roman Empire

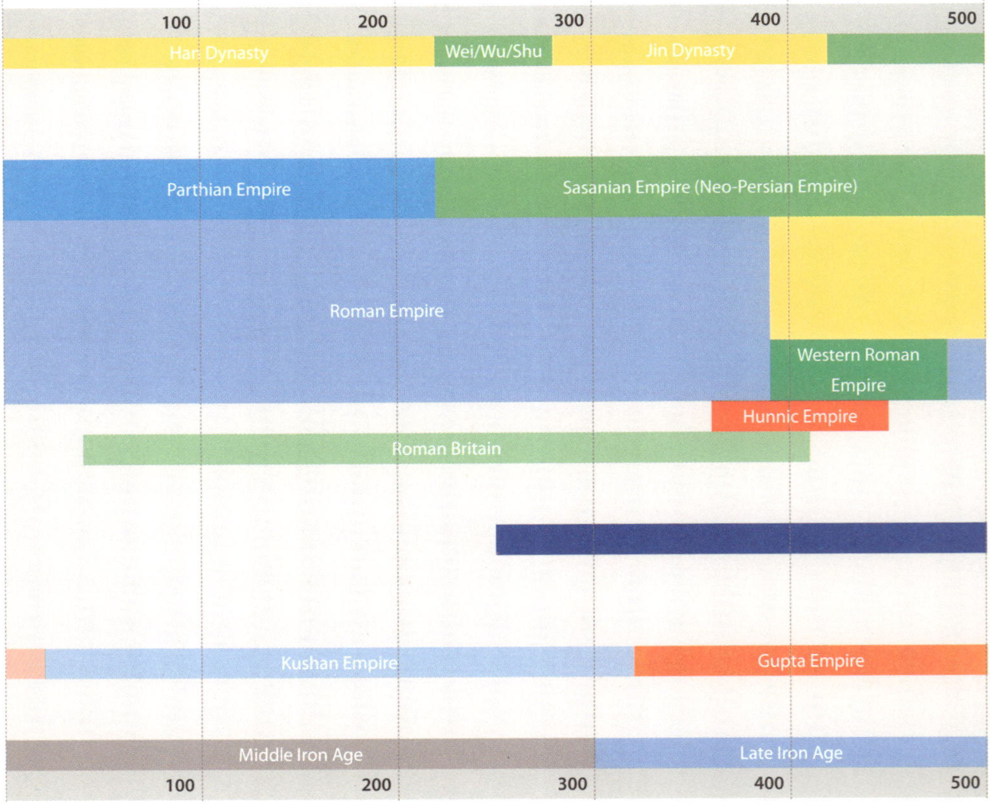
100
200
300
400
500
Han Dynasty
Wei/Wu/Shu
Jin Dynasty
Parthian Empire
Sasanian Empire (Neo-Persian Empire)
Roman Empire
Western Roman Empire
Hunnic Empire
Roman Britain
Kushan Empire
Gupta Empire
Middle Iron Age
Late Iron Age
100
200
300
400
500

600 700 800 900 1000

Muhammad (c. 570-632)

Pope Gregory I
(c. 540-604)

Charlemagne
(742-814)

Vikings Discover
America (1000)

Cordoba
Kairouan
Damascus
Kufa
Isfahan
Fustat
Medina
Mecca

Umayyad Caliphate (661-750)

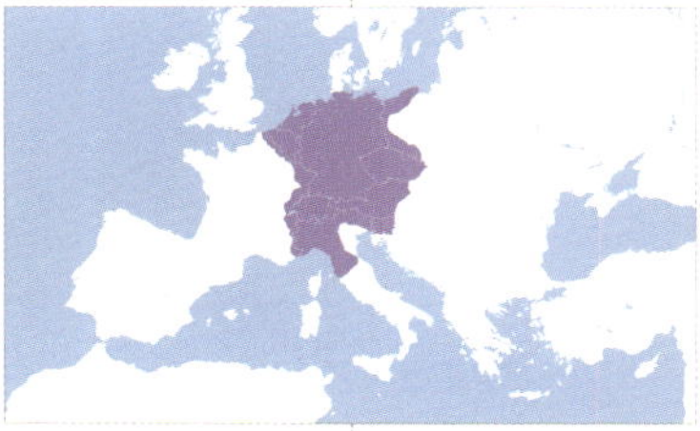

Holy Roman Empire (800-1806)

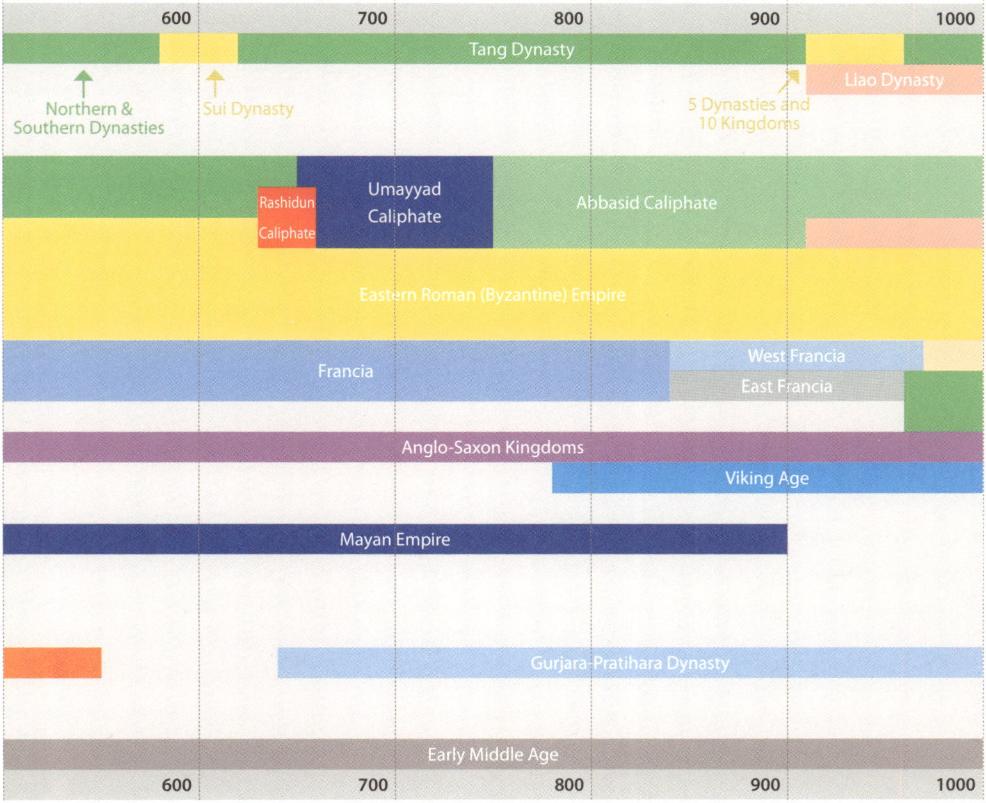
600
700
800
900
1000
Tang Dynasty
Northern &
Southern Dynasties
Sui Dynasty
5 Dynasties and
10 Kingdoms
Liao Dynasty
Rashidun
Caliphate
Umayyad
Caliphate
Abbasid Caliphate
Eastern Roman (Byzantine) Empire
Francia
West Francia
East Francia
Anglo-Saxon Kingdoms
Viking Age
Mayan Empire
Gurjara-Pratihara Dynasty
Early Middle Age
600
700
800
900
1000

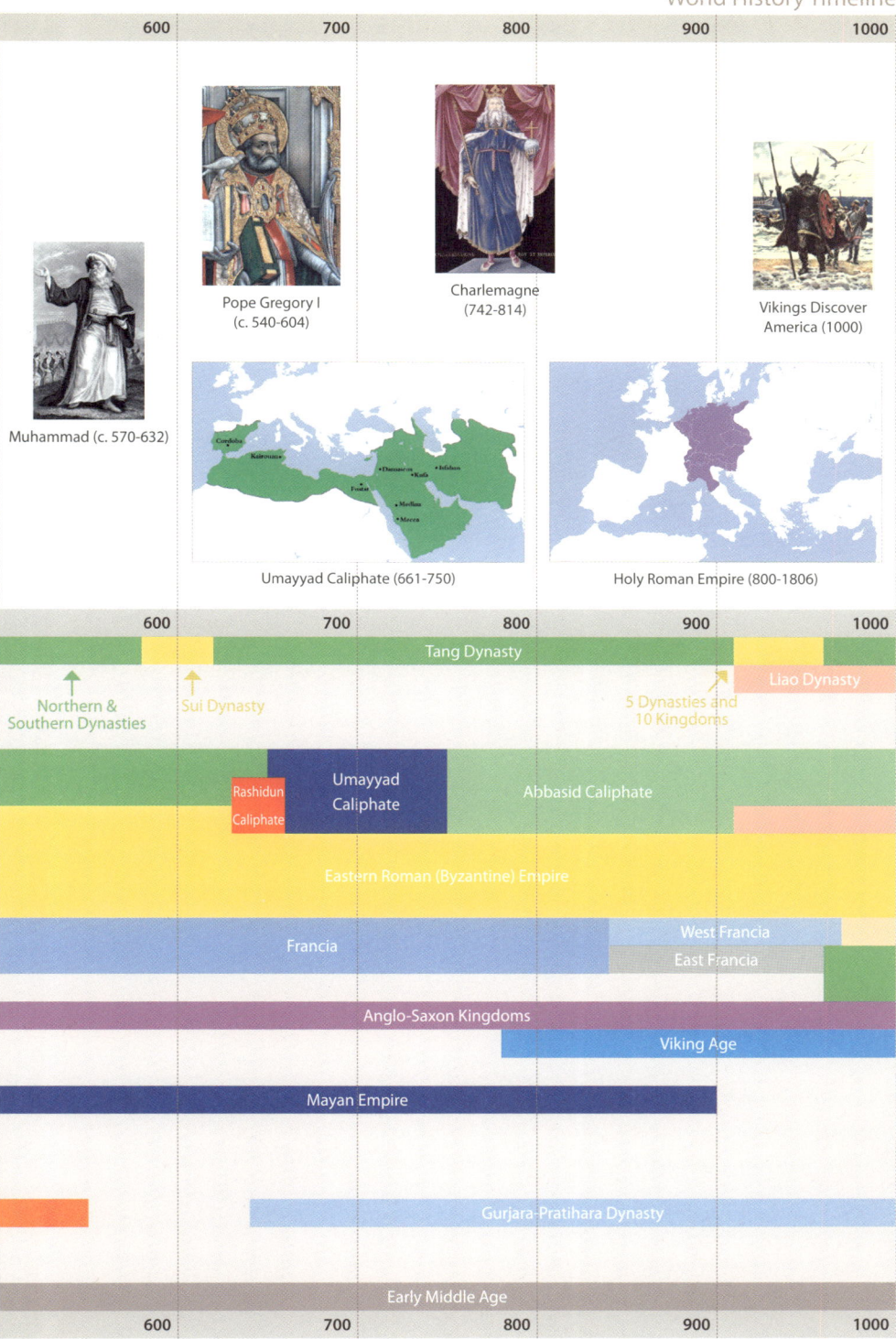

World History Timeline

1100 1200 1300 1400 1500

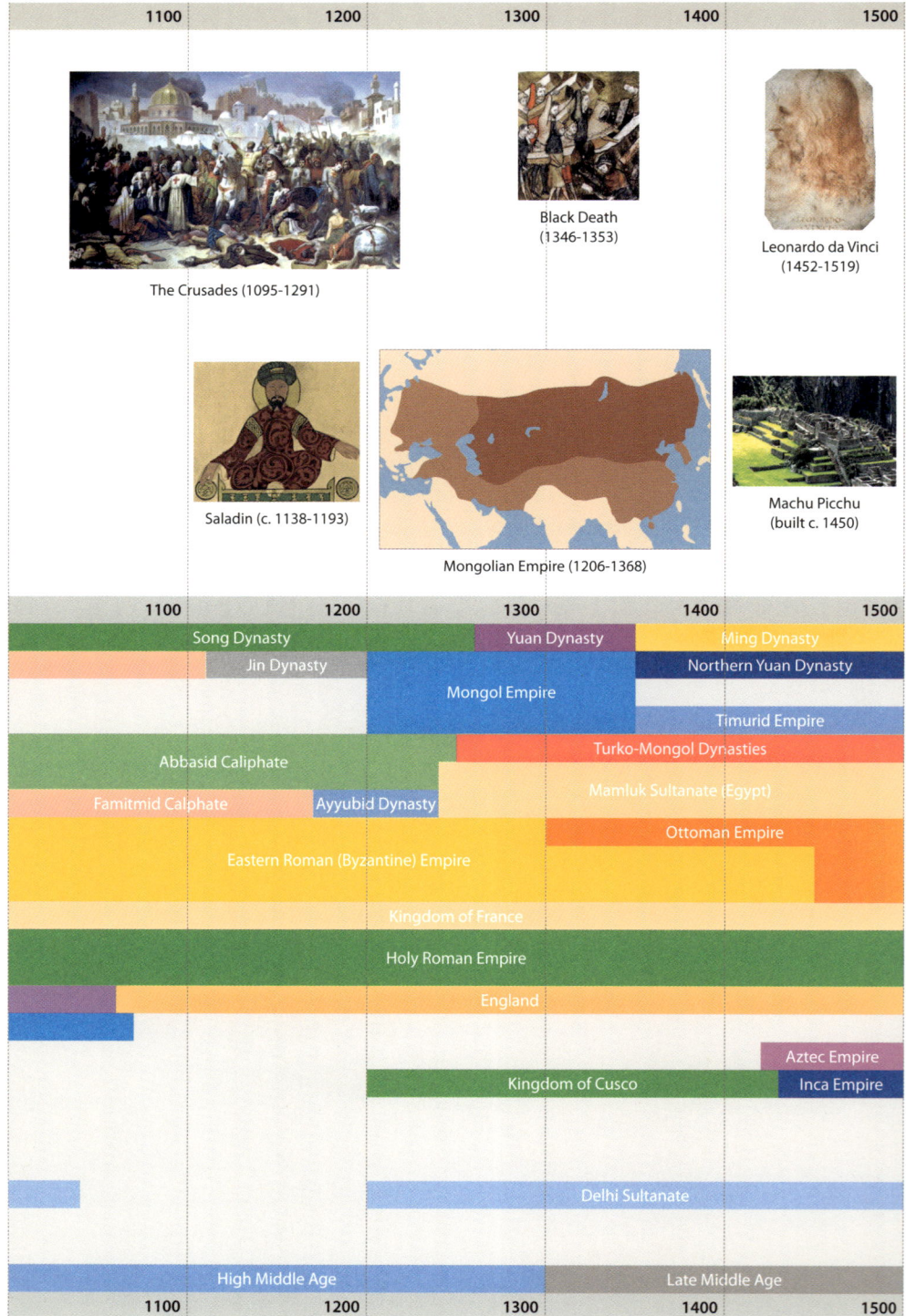

The Crusades (1095-1291)

Black Death (1346-1353)

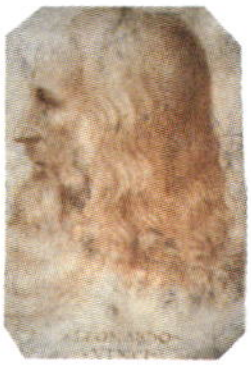

Leonardo da Vinci (1452-1519)

Saladin (c. 1138-1193)

Mongolian Empire (1206-1368)

Machu Picchu (built c. 1450)

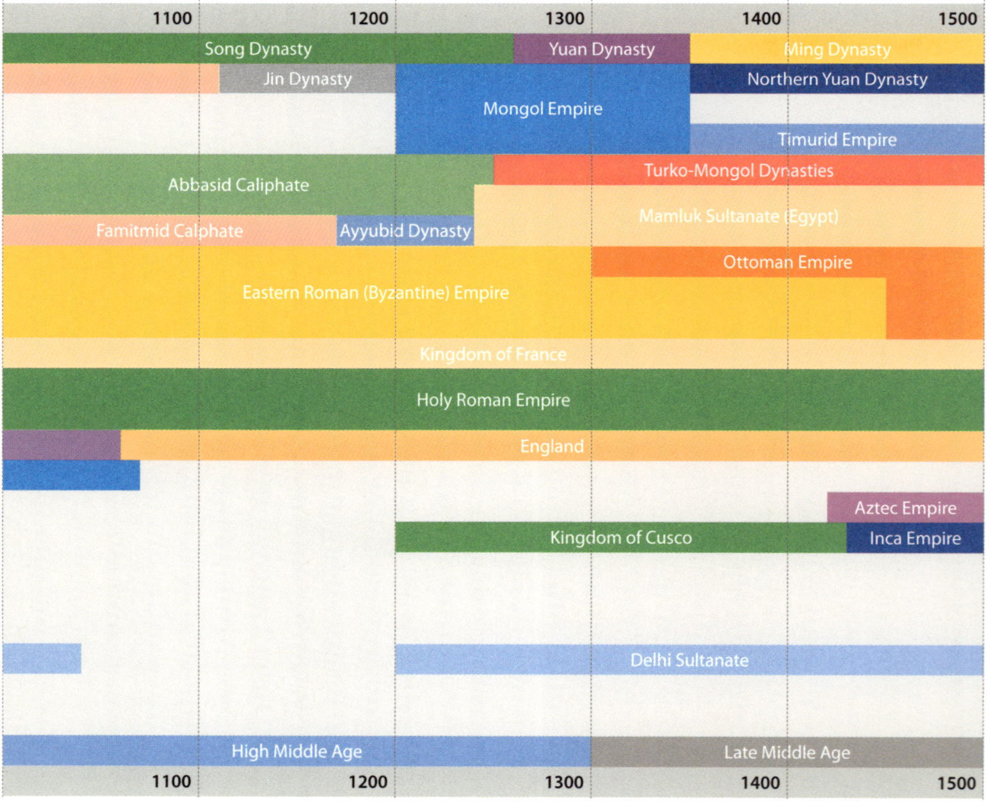
1100
1200
1300
1400
1500
Song Dynasty
Yuan Dynasty
Ming Dynasty
Jin Dynasty
Northern Yuan Dynasty
Mongol Empire
Timurid Empire
Turko-Mongol Dynasties
Abbasid Caliphate
Mamluk Sultanate (Egypt)
Famitmid Calphate
Ayyubid Dynasty
Ottoman Empire
Eastern Roman (Byzantine) Empire
Kingdom of France
Holy Roman Empire
England
Aztec Empire
Kingdom of Cusco
Inca Empire
Delhi Sultanate
High Middle Age
Late Middle Age
1100
1200
1300
1400
1500

1600 | 1700 | 1800 | 1900 | 2000

Taj Mahal (built 1653)

George Washington (1732-1799)

Battle of Waterloo (1815)

Suleiman the Magnificent (1494-1566)

Napoleon (1769-1821)

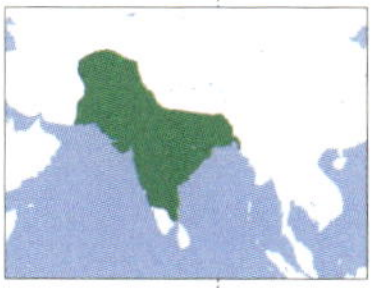
Mughal Empire (1526-1540 and 1555-1857)

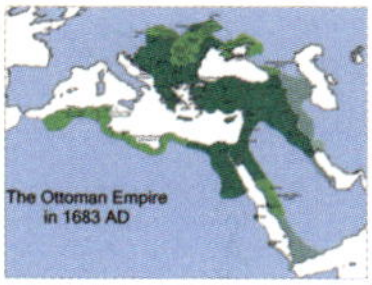
The Ottoman Empire
in 1683 AD
Ottoman Empire (1299-1922)

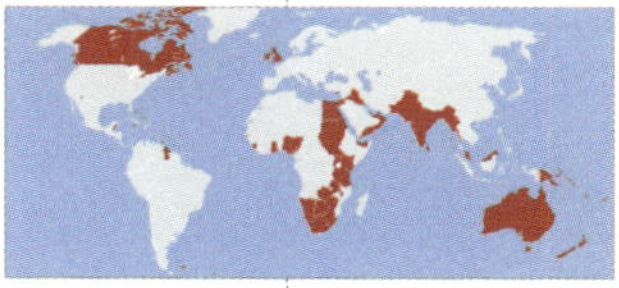
British Empire (1583-1997)

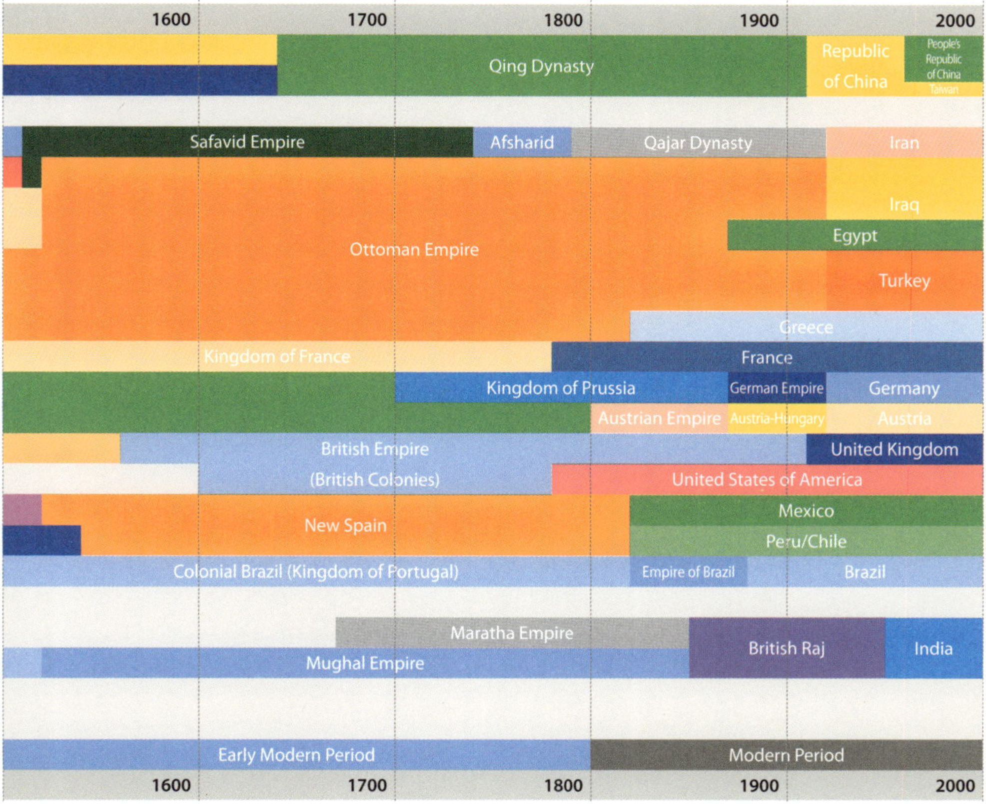
1600
1700
1800
1900
2000
Qing Dynasty
Republic of China
People's Republic of China
Taiwan
Safavid Empire
Afsharid
Qajar Dynasty
Iran
Iraq
Ottoman Empire
Egypt
Turkey
Greece
Kingdom of France
France
Kingdom of Prussia
German Empire
Germany
Austrian Empire
Austria-Hungary
Austria
British Empire
(British Colonies)
United Kingdom
United States of America
New Spain
Mexico
Peru/Chile
Colonial Brazil (Kingdom of Portugal)
Empire of Brazil
Brazil
Maratha Empire
Mughal Empire
British Raj
India
Early Modern Period
Modern Period
1600
1700
1800
1900
2000

List of Books

LEVEL 1

1. Calendars and the History of Time
2. Searching for El Dorado
3. The Tower of Babel
4. The Pilgrim Fathers
5. Traveling on the Silk Road
6. The Invention of Writing
7. The Making of a United Europe
8. The Magic of Numbers
9. The Persian Empire
10. The Great Wall of China

LEVEL 2

1. The Ottomans and Their Empire
2. The War Between the States
3. The Industrial Revolution
4. The Agricultural Revolution
5. Wars in the Middle East
6. The British Empire, Then and Now
7. The Neo-Assyrian Empire
8. The Rise and Fall of Communism
9. The History of Printing
10. The Vikings and Erik the Red

LEVEL 3

1. Space Exploration
2. The Spanish Conquest of the Americas
3. Cleopatra
4. The French Revolution
5. Benjamin Franklin
6. Galileo Galilei
7. The Battle of Salamis
8. Tea and Wars
9. Christopher Columbus
10. The Trojan War

LEVEL 4

1. Alexander the Great
2. Leonardo da Vinci
3. The Neo-Babylonian Empire
4. The Birth of the United States of America
5. Life and Death in Ancient Egypt
6. Life in the Roman Army
7. The Great Plane Race
8. Genghis Khan
9. Korea: A Land Divided by War
10. The Crusades

LEVEL 5

1. The Story of the Renaissance
2. The Great Plague
3. The Mughal Empire
4. Popes and Kings in the Middle Ages
5. Tutankhamun
6. The Story of the Reformation
7. The Medical Revolution
8. Decisive Battles of World War II
9. China: The New Superpower
10. The Great Depression

LEVEL 6

1. World War I
2. Communication Technology
3. The First Democracies
4. The Cold War
5. Global Trade and Peace
6. Greek Culture
7. Napoleon
8. The History of Transportation
9. Capitalism: Good or Evil?
10. China's First Empire: The Qin Dynasty